MW00958792

Chapters

ipromote

Introduction

You're a business owner. You know what it takes to succeed in your industry. Or you may be wondering why your seemingly genius business plan might not be panning out the way you always envisioned. Whether you've been in business for 50 years or 5 months; you need to acknowledge the influence of the digital age on the way business gets done and how consumer behavior drives revenue.

After doing business and finding success for digital advertisers in a highly competitive industry for over 20 years, iPromote has mastered the key to finding success in this cut throat industry. And we've written this guide to share the key to online growth.

Let's see if any of these scenarios sound familiar to you?

1. Larger sites and big box stores are driving up the costs of advertising and you're wondering how to win paid ad auctions to bring in quality leads.
2. You struggle to keep up with the evolving online search trends and needs of customers in order to be successful.

ipromote

3. Marketplace sites like Amazon drive down margins and enable increased competition for your business.
4. Client acquisition costs continue to increase year after year while you're just trying to stay operational and competitive.

What can be done to fix this cycle? For over 20 years, iPromote has mastered omni-channel advertising and adapted our proprietary platform to optimize advertising dollars for each platform. We've tracked, refined, and created solutions for thousands of small to medium sized ecommerce businesses, and talked with dozens of CEOs and business leaders to find what they do to set themselves apart. We know what it takes to succeed. And this book takes a look at what we've compiled from our learnings in order to set yourself up for success.

ipromote

Chapter 1

Identify the Obstacles & Know What You Can and Can't Handle

As seasoned experts in digital paid advertising, we've seen it grow and evolve dramatically over the years. We understand the unique challenges that ecommerce businesses face. Identifying these obstacles is the first critical step towards fostering growth and achieving success in the highly competitive digital marketplace.

Since you operate a business that relies heavily on the internet to drive leads and revenue, you might have a single person or a small team managing the website, social media, or other marketing efforts like email. Large companies can sustain an entirely in-house team. But for a majority of businesses like yours, it's not possible or the best solution for your business when it comes to identifying and overcoming the biggest obstacles you face. You simply can't do it all on your own, and that's ok. We want to help identify the biggest problems, so you know how to find the best solutions.

Take a look to see if any of these obstacles apply to your business.

ipromote

Understanding & Overcoming Market Saturation

One of the primary obstacles to growth for ecommerce businesses is market saturation. With countless competitors vying for the same audience, it becomes increasingly challenging to stand out.

Online marketplaces specifically present unique obstacles. One of the biggest obstacles is trying to drive traffic to your own ecommerce site when consumers become more and more reliant on the ease of sites like Amazon. You need to understand how your target audience shops, where they spend their time, and how they make their purchase decisions. That can help you set your best paid advertising strategy to drive traffic, customers, and revenue back to your business.

Do you know how to identify those opportunities?

Navigating Constraints

Budget constraints are a significant barrier for many businesses. Limited financial resources can restrict the scope and effectiveness of advertising campaigns. To identify budget-related obstacles, conduct a thorough audit of current ad spend versus revenue goals.

And as the number of platforms and marketing channels used for customer acquisition continues to grow, the ability to optimize and coordinate content across those channels is also important. Many invest in specially-designed software to make the process easier, or they pay a high licensing fee to have a popular system do it for them. Most small businesses can't afford these solutions, making outsourcing resources a more realistic option.

What places would you invest in your lead generation and revenue management if you didn't have to worry about the overhead cost?

Adapting to Changing Consumer Behavior

Consumer behavior is constantly evolving, and ecommerce businesses must adapt to these changes to stay relevant. Flexible and adaptable advertising solutions can enable quick pivots in strategies in response to shifting consumer preferences and market dynamics that shift to be more personalized and more consumer focused, rather than being driven by brand loyalty.

While the needed platforms vary from business to business and in different industries, there are key ones you'll always need to promote your business. Things like Google and social media platforms. But the strategies behind how to effectively manage the ad spend and navigate these platforms has changed. For in-house employees, this requires time and effort spent learning how to stay up-to-date.

Do your customers still act and shop in the same way they always have? Or do you need to make some changes to reach them effectively?

Key Questions

- *What tasks take up the most energy and time each week? Could outsourcing some of the important or technical-driven tasks help you accomplish more work focused on driving revenue?*
- *What tasks do you feel most qualified to handle? What could you potentially outsource to experts?*
- *What software or systems help you accomplish your most important tasks and work?*

ipromote

Chapter 2
Stop Focusing on Cost – Focus on Value

In the world of ecommerce, where margins can be tight and competition fierce, it's tempting to focus on cost-cutting measures. However, the true path to sustainable growth lies in prioritizing value and maximizing return on investment (ROI).

Understanding Value Over Cost

While cost control is important, it should never come at the expense of overall value to a business. The most successful businesses are those that invest in activities and resources that deliver the highest ROI. This means directing efforts and budgets towards strategies that generate the most revenue and enhance the customer experience. By focusing on value, and high-value tasks, businesses can create a more sustainable and scalable model for growth.

While cost control is important, it should never come at the expense of overall value to a business. The most successful businesses are those that invest in activities and resources that deliver the highest ROI. This means directing efforts and budgets towards strategies that generate the most revenue and enhance the customer experience. By focusing on value, and high-value tasks, businesses can create a more sustainable and scalable model for growth.

ipromote

Understanding Value Over Cost

While cost control is important, it should never come at the expense of overall value to a business. The most successful businesses are those that invest in activities and resources that deliver the highest ROI. This means directing efforts and budgets towards strategies that generate the most revenue and enhance the customer experience. By focusing on value, and high-value tasks, businesses can create a more sustainable and scalable model for growth.

While cost control is important, it should never come at the expense of overall value to a business. The most successful businesses are those that invest in activities and resources that deliver the highest ROI. This means directing efforts and budgets towards strategies that generate the most revenue and enhance the customer experience. By focusing on value, and high-value tasks, businesses can create a more sustainable and scalable model for growth.

Key Questions

- *What will it take to increase your sales by X% in the next 12 months?*
- *Given your current market position and budget, what activities will generate the highest ROI?*
- *What areas do you need to change to effectively compete in the marketplace and industry?*
- *What is a reasonable expectation of overall ROI on your current investments?*

◎ ipromote

Evaluating Potential Outsourcing Partners

Most of the time, these high value tasks can come at a price. You might not have the expertise or the staff to keep up with the latest marketing or business development opportunities. Outsourcing non-core tasks is a powerful strategy for maximizing value. By outsourcing these tasks to specialized providers, you can free up your internal resources to focus on what you do best. This not only improves efficiency but also ensures that these functions are handled by experts who can deliver high-quality results.

When considering outsourcing, it's crucial to evaluate potential partners carefully. Look for providers with a proven track record in their field, strong references, and the capability to scale with your business. Effective communication and alignment of goals are also essential to ensure a successful partnership. By choosing the right partners, you can enhance the quality and efficiency of your outsourced functions, contributing to overall business growth.

The term outsourcing can cause some anxiety with many. It's tough and can feel like you're letting go of control of your business. But having the right partner is actually just the opposite. Outsourcing can mean you're making a key strategic decision to bring more value to your business. The value you get from their services far outweighs the cost, and drives ROI.

Chapter 3 –
Set Clear Expectations

In our time in the marketing world, we've found two key reasons most partnerships or outsourcing relationships fail. That is a lack of specific deliverables and a lack of clear communications.

Setting clear expectations from the beginning of any partnership is fundamental to achieving mutual success. This involves defining specific goals, deliverables, timelines, and responsibilities. For any business, this clarity ensures that all parties are aligned and working towards the same objectives. Clear expectations help prevent misunderstandings, reduce conflicts, and create a roadmap for achieving desired outcomes.

When partnering with digital advertising experts or other service providers, it is essential to outline specific deliverables. These deliverables should be measurable, attainable, and relevant to your business goals. For instance, if you are running a PPC campaign, define the expected increase in website traffic, conversion rates, or sales. Detailed deliverables provide a benchmark against which you can measure progress and success, ensuring that all efforts are focused on achieving tangible results.

Maintaining Open Communication

Effective communication is the cornerstone of any successful partnership. Regular updates, feedback sessions, and transparent reporting are critical to maintaining a productive relationship. Establishing a communication plan that includes scheduled check-ins and performance reviews helps keep everyone on the same page. This ongoing dialogue should ensure any issues are promptly addressed and that the partnership remains aligned with evolving business needs.

Sometimes this looks like a monthly check in. Other times, it's regular viewings of a dashboard or project management board. Even things like shared calendars, and real-time messaging apps can streamline interactions and keep all stakeholders informed. For ecommerce businesses, these tools can help manage multiple partnerships simultaneously, ensuring that all projects stay on track and that deliverables are met on time.

Addressing Challenges and Adjusting Expectations

No partnership is without its challenges. When obstacles arise, it is important to address them promptly and adjust expectations as needed. Openly discussing any issues and working collaboratively to find solutions helps maintain trust and keeps the partnership productive. Being adaptable and responsive to changes in the market or project scope is crucial for sustaining long-term success.

ipromote

Recognizing and celebrating successes is an important aspect of maintaining a positive and motivated partnership. Regularly reviewing performance against the set deliverables and acknowledging achievements fosters a culture of continuous improvement. For ecommerce businesses, this practice not only strengthens partnerships but also drives ongoing innovation and growth.

Key Questions

- *How to quantify the work being done. What can I specifically count on being completed each month?*
- *What is the timetable for deliverables? What will I receive on an ongoing basis?*
- *What should my team prepare for before any meeting to make them as productive as possible?*

ipromote

Chapter 4 –
Learn How to Identify the Right Partner

Identifying the right partner for your ecommerce advertising needs is crucial for long-term success. With numerous agencies and vendors vying for your business, it's essential to distinguish the true experts from those who might overpromise and underdeliver.

Red Flags & Key Questions

One of the first red flags to watch out for is a lack of transparency. A reputable partner should be open about their methods, pricing structure, and performance metrics. They should provide clear, comprehensive reporting that gives you insight into how your advertising budget is being spent and what results are being achieved. Be wary of agencies that use vague language or seem reluctant to share detailed information about their processes.

When evaluating potential partners, it's important to ask the right questions. Inquire about their experience in your specific industry, their track record with businesses similar to yours, and their approach to strategy development. A strong partner should be able to provide case studies or references that demonstrate their ability to drive tangible results. Don't hesitate to ask about their team structure, the tools they use, and how they stay updated on the latest industry trends and platform changes.

Complete transparency in reporting is non-negotiable. Your advertising partner should offer real-time access to performance data and be willing to explain any discrepancies or unexpected results. Look for partners who use industry-standard reporting tools and can provide customized reports that align with your specific KPIs. A trustworthy partner will not only share successes but also be upfront about challenges and how they plan to address them.

Seeking Advice for Key Collaboration

Be cautious when seeking advice, especially if it seems too good to be true. While it's natural to want quick results, sustainable success in digital advertising often requires time and continuous optimization. Be skeptical of partners who guarantee specific impressions or promise immediate, dramatic increases in sales without a solid strategy to back up their claims. A reliable partner will set realistic expectations and focus on long-term growth rather than short-term gains.

Consider the partner's approach to collaboration and communication. The right partner should view your relationship as a true partnership, taking the time to understand your business goals and aligning their strategies accordingly. They should be proactive in their communication, regularly updating you on campaign performance and market trends. Look for a partner who is responsive to your questions and concerns, and who demonstrates a genuine interest in your business's success beyond just managing your ad spend.

Seeking Advice for Key Collaboration

Be cautious when seeking advice, especially if it seems too good to be true. While it's natural to want quick results, sustainable success in digital advertising often requires time and continuous optimization. Be skeptical of partners who guarantee specific impressions or promise immediate, dramatic increases in sales without a solid strategy to back up their claims. A reliable partner will set realistic expectations and focus on long-term growth rather than short-term gains.

Consider the partner's approach to collaboration and communication. The right partner should view your relationship as a true partnership, taking the time to understand your business goals and aligning their strategies accordingly. They should be proactive in their communication, regularly updating you on campaign performance and market trends. Look for a partner who is responsive to your questions and concerns, and who demonstrates a genuine interest in your business's success beyond just managing your ad spend.

You should always set proper communication loops with anyone you partner with.

1. A regular, scheduled call to review reports and discuss action items. It should always include relevant staff including marketing, sales, and leadership to make sure everyone's priorities are synced.
2. Set channels for any direct and impromptu communication. That could be email or phone calls. Be sure you know the best way to communicate for any future needs like launching a new product or need to make a change to your offering.

Key Questions

- *What experience do you have with the specific product or service I'm offering?*
- *What does your reporting dashboard look like?*
- *What's the best way to communicate regularly?*
- *Do the action items completely create a better experience for all parties including our end customer?*

Chapter 5 –

Setting the Steps to Success for Your Partnerships & Customers

In the ever-evolving ecommerce landscape, setting a clear path to success for both your partnerships and customers is crucial. As digital advertising experts, we understand the importance of establishing a structured approach to ensure that all stakeholders are aligned and working towards common goals.

Accelerate Work with Strategic Planning

A well-defined strategic plan is the foundation of accelerated work. Begin by outlining the overarching goals for your partnerships and projects. Identify key milestones and create a detailed timeline that outlines specific tasks and deadlines. By having a clear roadmap, your team can prioritize tasks, manage time effectively, and reduce the risk of delays. Regularly reviewing and adjusting the plan based on progress and new information ensures that your efforts remain focused and efficient.

From there, you can allocate resources as needed. Assess the strengths and weaknesses of your team and identify areas where external support may be needed. Allocate resources to high-priority tasks that align with your business's core competencies and strategic objectives. This may involve investing in advanced technology, hiring specialized talent, or partnering with experts who can provide additional support. By focusing resources on the most impactful areas, you can maximize efficiency and drive better outcomes.

Setting Monthly Benchmarks

Monthly benchmarks are essential for tracking progress and maintaining momentum. These benchmarks should be specific, measurable, and aligned with your overall goals. For example, if you're running a digital advertising campaign, set targets for key performance indicators (KPIs) such as website traffic, conversion rates, and return on ad spend (ROAS). Regularly reviewing these benchmarks allows you to identify trends, adjust strategies, and celebrate successes. It also provides an opportunity to address any challenges and make necessary adjustments to stay on track.

Open and transparent information sharing is vital for building trust and ensuring everyone is on the same page. Establish clear communication channels and protocols for sharing updates, reports, and data. This includes providing partners with access to real-time analytics, performance dashboards, and detailed reports. Transparency not only fosters accountability but also enables all stakeholders to make informed decisions. Ensure that all relevant information is easily accessible and that any questions or concerns are promptly addressed.

Encouraging Collaboration & Feedback

Collaboration is key to successful partnerships. Encourage open dialogue and active participation from all team members and partners. Regular meetings, brainstorming sessions, and collaborative tools can facilitate the exchange of ideas and foster a culture of continuous improvement. Additionally, seek feedback from your partners and customers to gain valuable insights into what's working well and where improvements can be made. This feedback loop is essential for refining processes and enhancing overall performance.

Documenting key milestones and achievements is an important step in tracking progress and celebrating success. Whether it's reaching a sales target, launching a new product, or completing a significant project, acknowledging these accomplishments boosts morale and reinforces the value of your partnerships. Share these successes with your team and partners to foster a sense of shared purpose and motivation. Celebrating milestones also provides an opportunity to reflect on lessons learned and set new goals for the future.

Continuous Monitoring & Improvement

The journey to success is ongoing. Continuously monitor the performance of your partnerships and projects, and be proactive in identifying areas for improvement. Stay informed about industry trends, emerging technologies, and best practices to ensure that your strategies remain relevant and effective. By embracing a mindset of continuous improvement, you can maintain a competitive edge and achieve long-term success in the dynamic ecommerce landscape.

Key Questions

- *Can you share examples of how you've adjusted plans mid-project to improve outcomes?*
- *What metrics do you track and how to you set benchmarks for success based on my overall project goals?*
- *How do you stay updated on industry trends, and how do you integrate new insights and technologies into your strategies?*
- *How do you ensure that you learn from both successes and challenges to drive continuous improvement?*

ipromote

About  ipromote

iPromote makes digital advertising accessible and affordable to every business through technology designed to service and support the unique needs of the SMB market.

We empower resellers to sell digital advertising efficiently and at scale through tools and technology built with an advanced level of automation to optimize ad spend on every channel. Our Demand Site Platform removes the middle man allowing ads to be placed on some of the biggest sites on the web directly from our platform.

Our Platform

Omni-Channel advertising maximizes your campaign reach. Or pick the channel you would like to focus on.

Our algorithm designs creative advertising in minutes using logos and colors from your website.

ipromote Platform

Pick your specific targeting locations. It can be local at 5 miles or nationwide!

We use AI to help you design the tone and text all your ads. Want to be conversational or more witty? Our platform can optimize the text of your ad for maximum conversion.

Ready to launch? You can view all your ads, and see the summary of your budget, locations, and everything else. before launch!

About Matt Tennison

Matt Tennison is CRO of iPromote and has over 25 years of experience in high level business development and partner/client management and SMB marketing. , With a rich background in print, direct response and performance-based advertising solutions for SMB's; Matt's current passion is online advertising. He specializes in driving revenue through high performing partner relationships, SMB strategy and digital product sales and value. He has helped build one of the biggest SMB SEO agencies in the world.

Matt enjoys spending time with his wife and 4 children and is a competitive road and gravel cyclist.

About Joe Parker

Joe Parker is the Director of Sales at iPromote. He joined the company after spending time as a top sales performer at the biggest home service marketing company in the United States, and also a team lead at the world's largest SEO provider for small business. He is passionate about solutions for small businesses that allow them to compete in today's world.

Outside of work, Joe is a father of 3 and has an MBA from the University of Utah.

ipromote

Made in the USA
Las Vegas, NV
25 November 2024

12600373R00015